MORE LIES ABOUT JERZY

Davey Holmes

BROADWAY PLAY PUBLISHING INC
New York
www.broadwayplaypublishing.com
info@broadwayplaypublishing.com

Cover art by Priscilla Holmes

First published in an earlier version in October 2002 in *Plays From The Vineyard Theatre*

This printing, revised: September 2018
I S B N: 978-0-88145-647-9

Book design: Marie Donovan
Page make-up: Adobe InDesign
Typeface: Palatino

MORE LIES ABOUT JERZY premiered at the Vineyard Theatre on 21 January 2001. The cast and creative contributors were:

JERZY .... Jared Harris
GEORGIA .... Gretchen Egolf
ISABEL .... Lizbeth Mackay
ARTHUR .... Daniel London
RYSIEK .... Boris McGiver
OSUCHA .... Betty Miller
KASIA .... Portia Reiners
BRETT, MR KERRY & YOUNG MAN .... Adam Stein
TALK-SHOW HOST, MR SORVILLO
   & JERZY'S FATHER .... Martin Shakar
HARRY FROTT & WITOLD TWAROG .... Gary Wilmes

Director .... Darko Tresnjak
Set design .... Derek McLane
Costume design .... Linda Cho
Lighting design .... Frances Aronson
Sound design .... Laura Grace Brown
Stage manager .... Katherine Lee Boyer

MORE LIES ABOUT JERZY was then produced in
London at New End Theatre (in association with
Framework Productions) from 22 October to 1
December 2002. The cast and creative contributors
were:

JERZY LESNEWSKI...................................... George Layton
ISABEL PARIS ....Karen Archer
GEORGIA FISCHER..................................Jacqueline Nairn
ARTHUR BAUSLEY.. Derek Hagen
HARRY, MR KERRY, WITOLD TWAROG...Richard Alleman
RYSIEK ZRUPINA ....Carl McCristal
BRETT, MR SORVILLA,
    MR LESNEWSKI................................Paul Vaughn Evans
MRS GRUSZKA, KASIA ....Natasha Oxley

Director...Guy Retallack
Stage manager.................................. Anne Schuermans
Designer................................... Nicolai Hart Hansen
Lighting..Oliver Fenwick
Sound ....Chris Branch & Tom Haines

MORE LIES ABOUT JERZY was subsequently
produced by Circus Theatricals (Jeannine Wisnosky,
Producer) at the Hayworth Theater in Los Angeles in
2010. The cast and creative contributor were:

JERZY .... Jack Stehlin
GEORGIA .... Kristin Malko
ISABEL .... Cameron Meyer
ARTHUR .... Adam Stein
RYSIEK.. Jordan Lund
BRETT .... Chet Grissom
HARRY FROTT...Neil Vipond

Director ....David Trainer

CHARACTERS & SETTING

JERZY LESNEWSKI, *30s or 40s*

GEORGIA FISCHER, *mid-20s*

ARTHUR BAUSLEY, *30s*

RYSIEK ZRUPINA

ISABEL PARRIS, *passes for 50*
OSUCHA GRUSZKA

HARRY FROTT
WITOLD TWAROG
MR KERRY

TALK-SHOW HOST
BRETT PEARSON
MR SORVILLO
YOUNG MAN
JERZY'S FATHER

(Minimum 5 men and 2 women, grouping above to suggest where actors can play multiple roles)

Time: 1972–1974

New York City

One

(Light on JERZY *in New York City, about 1972, standing in the wings of a live-audience T V talk show as he waits to go on. We hear the show in progress, muffled and distant, the host talking, the audience laughing. He dabs at perspiration on his forehead with a handkerchief, breathless with anxiety.)*

(Light on GEORGIA *in 1974. Direct address)*

GEORGIA: I met a woman who after ten seconds of conversation started sharing personal stories about herself. As a way of being friendly, I think. Except it felt obscene.

(Talk show music)

TALK-SHOW HOST: *(Recorded)* Our next guest is a Holocaust survivor and award-winning author, also known for putting on a phony beard and going to nightclubs—

*(*JERZY *walks upstage center and sits facing upstage. Immediately lights go up on* JERZY *and a* TALK SHOW HOST *having a televised conversation. The pair have their backs to the audience, sillhouetted as they face an invisible studio audience upstage. Dialogue between them is pre-recorded and tinny, like a T V playing in the next room.* JERZY's *demeanor has changed: he seems relaxed, funny, outrageous.)*

TALK-SHOW HOST: Jerzy, thanks for coming on the show.

JERZY: I'm admiring your jacket. Looks very soft.

TALK-SHOW HOST: It is soft.

(Laughter from the studio audience)

JERZY: Can I try it on?

(Laughter abruptly cuts out—)

(Light on HARRY *and* ISABEL *in 1974.)*

ISABEL: People talking about him, cocktail parties or—
you know, they drive me crazy. Reducing his entire
body of work to some phrase, some glib...

HARRY: Mm-hm.

ISABEL: When they don't know the first thing, clearly,
they're not even trying to understand him. He's this
topic that ostensibly makes them sound intelligent.

HARRY: Mm-hm.

ISABEL: All they know—all they know—

HARRY: They know what they read.

ISABEL: Exactly.

(Talk show continues.)

TALK-SHOW HOST: You were separated from your
parents as a child. Came over from Poland in your
twenties, without any money—

JERZY: I did have money. I had three dollars.

(Laughter cuts out—)

*(*GEORGIA *continues.)*

GEORGIA: My sister flipped through it before going
to bed. A scene where a boy is raped as a little girl
watches. A man being eaten alive by rats.

(Light on ARTHUR *in 1974. Direct address)*

ARTHUR: A beautiful book.

GEORGIA: She said, "What the hell *is* this? Not a
bedtime story." But I never said it was...

ARTHUR: I *always* said it was.

GEORGIA: I said, this is brilliant.

ARTHUR: And I went on record. One of the first.

(Talk show continues.)

TALK-SHOW HOST: You put on disguises at night and go to these clubs.

JERZY: Sex clubs.

TALK-SHOW HOST: Thought I'd let you tell them that!

(Laughter)

JERZY: Forget the book. Let's talk about New York nightlife, much more interesting.

(Laughter cuts out.)

(ARTHUR continues.)

ARTHUR: I wrote a positive review. Then Paul told me *Vantage Point* was autobiography, that these things *happened*. I went back to my review, changed the word "insightful" to "genius".

(HARRY and ISABEL continue.)

ISABEL: Honestly? I understand him as well as anyone. Not because I slept with him. I *did* sleep with him but…it's because Jerzy and I think alike, in many ways. You agree?

HARRY: I mean, I'm not…

ISABEL: Not what?

HARRY: I'm hardly objective. Am I.

(Talk show continues.)

TALK-SHOW HOST: You hear me reading my notes, describing your life. What goes through your mind?

JERZY: I think, who is he talking about? Is that me?

(Applause cuts out—)

(GEORGIA *continues.*)

GEORGIA: I never talk to anyone now. Really talk. But I'm sure I will. At some point.

Two

(BRETT, HARRY, ISABEL *and* JERZY *in* ISABEL'*s apartment. Even under attack,* BRETT *and* HARRY *enjoy the performance.*)

JERZY: *(To* BRETT *and* HARRY*)* You are vultures, both of you.

ISABEL: That's not nice.

JERZY: Better they hear it from a friend, save them from shock. One day Harry wakes up, thinks: my God, I hate myself. I am a philistine, a scavenger living on bloody scraps, robbing artists of their unique—etcetera. You admit?

HARRY: That I'm a scavenger?

BRETT: Or that he hates himself.

HARRY: Both, but don't try to distract us from—

ISABEL: *(Overlapping)* He is, he's attacking so you'll forget what you were—

JERZY: *(Overlapping)* I'm not, I'm not! Look: I can sound like an idiot on T V without your help. That you have hired an idiot to tell me—

ISABEL: *He* didn't hire—

JERZY: He didn't stop them. *(Crosses to bottle of wine)* Everyone needs a *publicist.* So you say. But the man they brought in, this paradigm, an expert on… *(To* ISABEL*)* Empty. *(Continues)* …an expert on appearance. When he himself makes people nauseous? People meet him, their impulse is to physically hurt him. Strike him.

(They laugh.)

JERZY: And he's giving me advice. Like a dentist with rotten teeth or—

HARRY: Imagine being Jerzy's publicist.

ISABEL: You'd have white hair within a week—

JERZY: *(Overlapping)* He sent me a list! Topics to avoid during interviews, things I should not bring up.

HARRY: Here we are, trying to push your book about the *Holocaust*, for God's sake, then last night on the talk show you went on about— *(To* BRETT*)* Did you see this? *(To* JERZY*)* The stuff about sex clubs. I've got nothing against sex clubs, they sound great but do you need to—

JERZY: Only in the sheltered minds of Americans do you have to be a saint to be a victim.

BRETT: Oh I like that.

JERZY: I chew with my mouth open, I shame the memory of murdered Jews? I do not *represent* the Jewish faith. I do not even represent my writing. Is there more wine?

HARRY: I can't get a word in, here—

ISABEL: *(Overlapping)* Help yourself, it's in the kitchen.

JERZY: The other night at a club, there was a man masturbating.

ISABEL: Ah.

JERZY: He had a huge…

HARRY: See, that's exactly what—

JERZY: *(Overlapping)* He did! And he was masturbating. I was with the Vice President of the Rotary Club. Very conservative, polite. We started talking to this man. Finally I wanted to go, but my friend thought it would be rude if we left before the man had an orgasm.

(They laugh.)

JERZY: You see, you enjoy that. Why can't you trust me to decide what people want? I've come this far.

HARRY: That's true, and we generally have no problem with, with shock value or— Really it's you who doesn't trust *us*. Look at any public figure, they all have help.

BRETT: Especially if there's a political element.

ISABEL: When I think about Nixon! All that talk about ending the war, he gets into office and does exactly the opposite. Now he's running for another term—

JERZY: *(Overlapping)* So you compare me to Nixon? How can you—

ISABEL: Shush!

(ISABEL holds her hand up. For a moment, the rush of conversation stops.)

ISABEL: Thought I heard the buzzer.

BRETT: Are you expecting someone?

HARRY: She won't tell us who. It's a surprise.

ISABEL: Jerzy's known them for years. That's all I'm going to say.

JERZY: From New York? Or…?

ISABEL claps a hand over her mouth.

JERZY: This is what she does, everything becomes an "event".

ISABEL: I do it to give our lives meaning. In lieu of genuine meaning.

(ISABEL hands BRETT a thin booklet.)

ISABEL: You haven't seen this.

BRETT: No! I was told you wrote poetry.

ISABEL: It's only a vanity press. Copies for friends.

BRETT: Still.

JERZY: On the back, look at her picture. She looks good, eh? It was taken thirty years ago but—

ISABEL: Jerzy! It's not *that* old!

JERZY: An artist has to define herself, which is what I've been saying. We all love Isabel, and we love her for wanting to be this…matriarch. With colorful scarves, famous friends and lovers—

ISABEL: Famous lovers? Just because I have *taste*. (*To* BRETT) I throw a party, next morning Jerzy will be gone and I'm vacuuming around his latest conquest, sprawled naked on the floor like a broken party favor.

BRETT: You deny this?

JERZY: Of course.

ISABEL: (*Strokes* JERZY's *cheek*) We're a good team, aren't we.

(JERZY *kisses* ISABEL's *hand*.)

JERZY: We certainly—

(*Door buzzer*)

ISABEL: Aha! (*She exits*.)

BRETT: What's her poetry like? (*A beat. Reading*) "The early light of my arousal / a golden warmth which—"

HARRY: Stop it.

JERZY: I feel great. Why don't we all go out with this mystery friend.

HARRY: Last week she had Tennessee Williams over.

BRETT: No kidding! I'd love to meet—

(ISABEL *re-enters with* RYSIEK.)

ISABEL: So.

(They all stand and turn. JERZY *doesn't react. An awkward pause)*

RYSIEK: You remember?

JERZY: Yes.

RYSIEK: Rysiek.

JERZY: Of course.

RYSIEK: Rysiek Zrupina.

JERZY: Right.

*(*RYSIEK *holds out his hand;* JERZY *woodenly shakes it.)*

RYSIEK: It's been a long time. I did not know if I would meet you again.

JERZY: But here we are.

RYSIEK: Here we are.

JERZY: Fantastic.

RYSIEK: *(Pause)* Rysiek from Krasnystaw.

JERZY: I remember. *(Pause)* I'm going to get more wine. Anyone need more wine?

ISABEL: *(To* RYSIEK*)* Would you…like some?

RYSIEK: Please.

*(*JERZY *exits.)*

BRETT: Hm. That was…

HARRY: It was, wasn't it.

ISABEL: *(Quickly)* Everyone, this is Rysiek. He, I think he knew Jerzy back in Poland.

BRETT: Wonderful.

ISABEL: I invited him over tonight, since… *(To* RYSIEK*)* Jerzy's book is being made into a movie and we're celebrating.

RYSIEK: Ah. *(Then)* He was not happy to see me.

HARRY: He was just startled.

ISABEL: This is Harry, Jerzy's literary agent.

HARRY: Hi.

ISABEL: And Brett is producing the movie.

RYSIEK: Very good.

ISABEL: *(Pause)* Why don't I check on him... *(She exits.)*

HARRY: So. You know Jerzy.

RYSIEK: Yeah.

BRETT: I take it you're a fan of his work.

RYSIEK: Oh yes.

BRETT: He's brilliant. Absolutely brilliant.

RYSIEK: His book *Vantage Point*. I read some tonight before I come here.

HARRY: Which part?

RYSIEK: Ah... The boy, he walk all night and he come to a village, okay? Which is empty he think. But there is a girl, she is watching. She point at him. And some boys run out, they grab him—

BRETT: *That* scene!

HARRY: God, what a brutal—

BRETT: I used it in the pitch. *(To* RYSIEK*)* When we sold the story to the studio. It was touch and go, I mean... Polish people, Holocaust. It's been done.

HARRY: "It's been done." For Christ's sake—

BRETT: No, I mean, this is how *they* think. So I said, listen. A little girl stands there while a group of boys try to *rape* him!

RYSIEK: This girl. Kasia—

BRETT: Kasia, right. Kasia's cheering them on.

HARRY: Not a Disney movie...

BRETT: Uh-uh. And they're gonna cut that part. But at the time it was magic—

RYSIEK: Kasia is my cousin.

(Light on ISABEL *and* JERZY *in the hallway of* ISABEL'*s apartment.* JERZY *is holding his coat.)*

ISABEL: You're not going home. It's ten o'clock.

JERZY: Isabel! Some of these Poles are nationalist, extremist, revisionist anti-Semites who want me dead. You should feel no compulsion to bring them into my social life.

ISABEL: Darling, I never meant to make you uncomfortable. I've heard you mention Rysiek—

JERZY: When?

ISABEL: Some story. You were swimming together. No? Something.

JERZY: I never said I *liked* him.

ISABEL: You did.

JERZY: Not with any sincerity! *(Then)* How…

ISABEL: He lives in Brooklyn. There was an article on you in some Polish magazine, Tomasz read it to me and there was a line about Rysiek. I thought it would be fun. Also, for Brett to meet an authentic Polish peasant, talk about…farming onions or… It was a bad idea. *(Then)* So is the night ruined?

*(*JERZY *hesitates, then takes off his coat. They rejoin* HARRY, BRETT *and* RYSIEK *in the next room.)*

HARRY: …And here he is.

*(*ISABEL *hands a glass of wine to* RYSIEK.*)*

ISABEL: What are we discussing?

*(*HARRY *looks at* BRETT.*)*

BRETT: Rysiek was just telling us, he's related to the girl in Jerzy's book. The one from the rape scene.

ISABEL: What?

HARRY: That's what he's saying.

JERZY: *(Laughs)* No, no. My friend. How could you think…?

RYSIEK: There is only one Kasia in Krasnystaw.

JERZY: Why are people always convinced *they* were the inspiration for every—

RYSIEK: There is only one—

JERZY: You didn't know this Kasia.

RYSIEK: Not as you know her, but—

JERZY: *(Lightly) Nikt sie nie martwi co ty pamietasz.*

(JERZY is smiling, but RYSIEK looks shocked. A long pause)

BRETT: *(To fill the silence)* It's a kick, isn't it? Bumping into someone you go this far back with.

HARRY: Sure.

BRETT: A guy I saw recently, he remembered my mother making sandwiches and drawing animals with the mustard. Animals with the mustard, I mean…!

ISABEL: I've got someone like that. We grew up together.

HARRY: The same woman who…?

(ISABEL nods.)

HARRY: How is she?

ISABEL: *(To the group)* Harry recommended a doctor. My friend has cancer, so…

BRETT: That's tough.

ISABEL: It's changed how she sees herself. She says cancer isn't sexy, death isn't sexy. We reminisce about how *wild* she used to be. She loves that.

HARRY: She's lucky to have you.

ISABEL: The new medicine makes her dreamy, makes her fantasize about…being young, I think.

BRETT: We all have an arc. Every good movie has an arc, so do…

(A beat)

RYSIEK: I tell you something, okay? No one in our village had, ah…sweet, you drink… Hot chocolate!

ISABEL: This was when?

RYSIEK: During the war. So, I am outside with Jerzy and my brother, okay? We smell this… So good! From where? We don't know. *(He holds his wine out in front of him and uses a hand to wave an imaginary hot chocolate scent to his nostrils.)* The smell is stronger. We hear someone coming. Then, hey! We see—

*(*JERZY *slaps the wineglass out of* RYSIEK's *hand.)*

ISABEL: Jerzy!

JERZY: *Toe sa moi przyjaciele! Rozumiesz? Nikt sie nie martwi co ty pamietasz, toe sa moi przyjaciele!*

(A pause. RYSIEK *gets his coat.)*

RYSIEK: Excuse me.

*(*ISABEL *starts to follow* RYSIEK *to the door, but he stops her.)*

RYSIEK: It's alright. I can…

*(*RYSIEK *exits. A pause)*

JERZY chuckles, dismissing the moment as a prank.

JERZY: Sorry.

Three

(Lights up on ARTHUR's *office.* ARTHUR, GEORGIA*)*

ARTHUR: One of the most important writers of the decade, or the century—I mean, arguably—

GEORGIA: I agree.

ARTHUR: You think of Conrad, Kafka, Nabakov maybe, that undercurrent of sexual, political—

GEORGIA: The interview went well?

ARTHUR: My tape ran out.

GEORGIA: Oh no!

ARTHUR: I was writing like— *(Mimes his desperation)* Didn't want to miss a word. I took a dozen pages of notes— Nice scarf.

GEORGIA: My…? Oh. Thank you.

ARTHUR: Looked everything over at home, what I had down. It's amazing how magnetic he is, the level of charisma—

GEORGIA: I've been rereading his books. The cruelty—

ARTHUR: Yeah.

GEORGIA: He makes it poetic, but the emotional part…

ARTHUR: …is hidden.

GEORGIA: You don't know what he's feeling.

ARTHUR: That you would say that…you specifically cause I think you distance yourself from…other people. But you observe. Don't you. You're quiet but the gears are turning.

GEORGIA: The gears—?

ARTHUR: *Vantage Point* is about an outsider looking in. Like me. Not to project but—I cover stories, people who've had things *happen* to them, people caught up in the whole…the swing of the whole… This city's a river washing past and I'm not in it. You feel that way?

GEORGIA: I guess…

ARTHUR: And when you read the book, a part of you— hold on, there's a… You've got a string. *(He seizes a string dangling from her scarf.)*

GEORGIA: It'll unravel—

ARTHUR: I'll burn it off. *(Produces a lighter)* Hold still.

GEORGIA: Wait.

(GEORGIA takes the scarf off and hands it to ARTHUR.)

ARTHUR: I'm saying he withholds emotion to provoke us or…

GEORGIA: Hard to tell what's provocation and what's really his—

ARTHUR: *(Having burned the thread)* Done.

GEORGIA: Thank you… I'm saying… *(Then)* Some of the facts in your article don't check out.

(A beat)

ARTHUR: What?

GEORGIA: I'm not done but I thought I should show you.

ARTHUR: They're running it Sunday.

(GEORGIA hands ARTHUR a copy of the article marked up with red pencil. He sets the scarf on the desk and reads.)

GEORGIA: Nothing serious. A couple dates.

ARTHUR: Why is *this* circled?

GEORGIA: He says he was separated from his parents a month before the Nazis turned Lodz into a ghetto. Which would be January.

ARTHUR: Right.

GEORGIA: In his biography, he said it was September first.

ARTHUR: Which bio, the authorized…?

GEORGIA: S L Ryson.

ARTHUR: So he made a mistake. It wasn't a month before the Nazis came, it was…five… Shit, I better call him.

GEORGIA: There are a few other—

ARTHUR: You'll have it checked by tomorrow?

GEORGIA: Sure.

ARTHUR: *(Off his watch)* Almost noon. Why don't we go over this at lunch? Grab a table at—

GEORGIA: I'd better not.

(Lights on ARTHUR *and* GEORGIA, *they face out.)*

ARTHUR: Whether or not I found her attractive—I mean she is attractive. I'd offer to take her to lunch, but at *work*. That's not asking someone out.

GEORGIA: Arthur did ask me out. There was always some pretense. Research we should do together, an opportunity to go along while he covered a story. Whatever it was, I'd make some vague excuse. He wasn't pushy.

ARTHUR: She was shy and to be honest, it was holding her back professionally. Which I understand, I mean I give all my time to my work. So she and I had a…I tried to get her more involved and—*anyway. (A beat)* It's irrelevant. Whether or not…whether or not I—

(Doorbell)

Four

(Lights up on JERZY'*s apartment. He enters in his underwear, having just woken up. He shouts through the door.)*

JERZY: Hello?

ARTHUR: Jerzy, It's Arthur. I should've called.

JERZY: Arthur Bausley?

ARTHUR: I wanted to talk—

JERZY: *(Throwing the door open)* My friend!

*(*ARTHUR *enters and notices* JERZY *isn't dressed.)*

ARTHUR: I woke you up.

JERZY: It's a beautiful day and I would have missed it completely.

ARTHUR: I can come back…

JERZY: Good to see you.

*(*JERZY *startles* ARTHUR *by giving him a hug.)*

JERZY: Your article was wonderful. A big success.

ARTHUR: Glad you think so.

JERZY: Excuse me… *(He makes a beeline for the bathroom. Exiting)* I talked to one of the editors, Paul Ferryman, a good friend of mine—

ARTHUR: You know Mister Ferryman?

JERZY: *(Offstage)* He agrees that you have real talent!

ARTHUR: Thank you.

(We hear JERZY *pissing.* ARTHUR *immediately starts looking around; he pokes his head into the kitchen, doubles back and moves towards the bedroom.)*

JERZY: *(Offstage)* They're hiring another critic soon. You're at the top of their list!

(The toilet flushes. JERZY *enters and begins gathering up various items of his clothing which lie scattered around the room.)*

JERZY: Pardon me while I straighten up.

ARTHUR: Was there anything about the article that bothered you?

JERZY: No. *(Then)* Well...maybe one, small...

ARTHUR: Please.

JERZY: *(Putting on his shirt)* Your job is to present facts in some sort of coherent order so people can form their own opinion of...whatever you're writing about. And you're careful how you do this. Very careful.

ARTHUR: You think I'm—?

JERZY: A little dry, which is not always bad. As a reader I *trust* you, you reek of objectivity. But...Lesnewski, born here, did that... There was room for more mystery! You can avoid imposing an opinion and still leave a taste of something drifting in the air. Inference. No... *(Pauses with one pantleg on)* Possibility. Details are there for their own sake, fine, or they are arranged as a question mark. Because life is possibility.

ARTHUR: I'm not sure I—

JERZY: A woman is standing fifty feet away, a stranger, you can't see her face. Next thing you know, you're using both fists to wash her menstrual blood out of your sheets. What does it mean? *(Pause)* Exactly! There are no words for it. And maybe there is more to your subject, in this case me, than can be conveyed with a fact. The article is fine, it's a small point but—

ARTHUR: I'm worried it wasn't dry enough.

*(*JERZY *looks at* ARTHUR.*)*

ARTHUR: You've read my reviews. I'm a fan, I was one of the first, but...you're aware some of the dates you gave me conflict with your biography. *(Then)* My research assistant assured me it was the biography which was incorrect. That you hadn't even *seen* the bio until it was published—

JERZY: That's right! I was furious. Ryson is dyslexic, he almost misspelled my name on the—

ARTHUR: Ryson claims he gave you the manuscript. And that you made changes. *(Then)* Many changes.

JERZY: Mm. *(Pause)*

I got it wrong, then or now—I don't know, one or the other, does it matter? The exact date. The reference point for, what, something that happened to me—

ARTHUR: You didn't tell me you're in arbitration with the Authors Guild.

JERZY: You care?

ARTHUR: I do.

JERZY: A proof-reader claims, and how this would happen I'm not sure, that I tricked him into writing my book and took credit. Or something like that.

ARTHUR: So you arranged for an interview with a journalist who's gone on record as a fan—

JERZY: It wasn't that mercenary. It was an interview. I sat with you and tried to conjure a stream of lurid detail, my life. An unsound element or two flew past. I didn't notice, it wasn't important—

ARTHUR: But it *is!* To me it's very important. That everything be factual.

JERZY: Yes. I apologize.

(A beat)

ARTHUR: Your book is, it's stunning. I hate to annoy you with this sort of—

JERZY: What else?

ARTHUR: *(Hesitates)* My research assistant. Her name is Georgia. She assured me she'd straightened it out. I've worked with her before, she's usually very thorough and... Are you sleeping with her?

(JERZY is startled.)

JERZY: Am I...? What makes you think we've even met?

ARTHUR: I don't know you well enough to be...prying into your...I hope you're not offended. It's just, there were indications.

JERZY: Are you serious?

ARTHUR: I should never have brought it up...

JERZY: You're dating this woman?

ARTHUR: No.

JERZY: In love with her.

ARTHUR: No, no, I'm...I respect her. I mean I like her, but it's a friendly... *(Then)* So you're not sleeping with her?

JERZY: I'm not.

ARTHUR: I can't believe I... Forgive me.

JERZY: Well now I'm interested. Maybe you could introduce us?

(Their laughter is cut short as GEORGIA *enters from the bedroom.)*

JERZY: That's it, wait until you hear me lie, *then* come out. *(Then)* I'm making coffee. Would either of you...?

ARTHUR: Yes please.

(JERZY exits. A pause)

GEORGIA: I wasn't sure how to bring it up. That I was...

ARTHUR: Right.

GEORGIA: Because, this is my personal life.

ARTHUR: I agree.

GEORGIA: *(Pause)* But I'm sorry if I—

ARTHUR: Hey, look, it's…

(ARTHUR *holds a hand up to keep* GEORGIA *from continuing. He goes to the couch and sits.)*

(A beat)

Five

(JERZY *is pouring a glass of water as slowly as possible, deliberately irritating* KERRY, *an arbiter for the Authors Guild.* SORVILLO *enters, the more sympathetic of the two arbiters.)*

KERRY: Let's get started.

(KERRY *waits for* JERZY *to finish drinking and set the glass down.)*

KERRY: You don't mind if we tape this? So we have a record of exactly what…

JERZY: Good.

(KERRY *places a tape recorder on the table.)*

KERRY: Then there's no disagreement about…

JERZY: Absolutely. And I'll do the same. *(Produces his own tape recorder)* So I'm clear on what we don't disagree about.

KERRY: *(Hits "record")* Meeting with Jerzy Lesnewski regarding Authors Guild of America arbitration case number two-six-five-zero.

JERZY: *(Hits "record")* Meeting with me regarding Oscar's ridiculous charges. And he's not even here to accuse me personally. Because he's a coward.

KERRY: *(To* SORVILLO) You have the…?

(SORVILLO *hands* KERRY *a piece of paper.*)

KERRY: Mister Duffy claims he worked with you on your book *The Vantage Point* and that, quote: "his contributions were often creative in nature."

JERZY: The word for this, I think, is bullshit.

KERRY: He did work with you…

JERZY: No.

KERRY: I thought we'd established—

JERZY: He worked *for* me. I hired him. Oscar was a student, he needed money, so—

SORVILLO: In what capacity would you say he… In your opinion.

JERZY: He'd collate, proof-read, check spelling. Look for repetitions. If I wrote: "the woman stood up", then later she stood up again, when did she sit down? That kind of thing.

SORVILLO: Proof-reading.

JERZY: It wasn't until it won the National Book Prize that he realized he'd written it all himself.

KERRY: Mister Duffy wasn't exactly a student…

JERZY: When I met him—

KERRY: An assistant professor of English. Not someone you'd usually hire to, you know? Collate papers.

JERZY: This brilliant man. Assistant professor. Why doesn't he write his own books? With his name on them. If checking spelling is such a waste of his talent—

KERRY: I'm sorry, would you… If you could move back in your seat, so the tape picks up your… For the record. (*Then*) If you'd repeat what you just…

JERZY: *(Leaning over the recorder)* Oscar…hasn't…
ritten…anything.

SORVILLO: Maybe what you consider proof-reading, he
feels is… That it's a question of definition.

JERZY: Maybe he thinks if he adds a comma, the
sentence is his!

SORVILLO: I'm just saying…

JERZY: You own a painting, your maid comes in and
dusts it. Now she should sign her name?

(KERRY clears his throat.)

KERRY: *(Reading)* "Lesnewski would tell me to *poeticize
that,* or *make it flow.* This was my cue to write the
passage from scratch." He's saying, essentially, you
had him construct—

JERZY: Impossible, and I'll tell you why. Because my
book was already written.

SORVILLO: It was…

JERZY: In conversations with my friends, and in letters.
Because each chapter is a piece of my life. Not his,
mine. How could he write it? Did he live my life?

KERRY: The incidents you describe, things which
happened to this boy…

JERZY: Yes…

KERRY: A lot of it's metaphorical. *(Then)* I mean it's not
entirely autobiography. You were separated from your
parents, like the boy, but some incidents…

JERZY: Are metaphorical.

KERRY: No?

JERZY: *(Pause)* My father is coming to visit, he's never
been to America. It's exciting for me, I think for him
too.

KERRY: I'm not sure I…

JERZY: Before the war, my family had a reunion. I was pretty young, but I remember, there were two hundred people. Two hundred. And a few years later, only four of them alive. So, I think maybe it's a metaphor. For something. All those people killed, it must represent… what? Because the thing itself is too simple. There must be more. Maybe you can tell me?

(A beat)

KERRY: Mister Lesnewski. You're absolutely right, it's not for me to… *(Pause)* I'll restrict my questions to the writing process, and leave the content to you.

Six

(JERZY's office. ISABEL seated and typing furiously. He paces as he dictates, holding a blue notebook.)

JERZY: New paragraph. A brief description of The Woman. Brown hair, early twenties… *(He peers over her shoulder, reading the page she's typing. Points)* This bit. You like it?

ISABEL: Which, here? It's good.

JERZY: Choppy.

ISABEL: We can go back…

JERZY: See if you can smooth it out. Take a minute.

ISABEL: Smooth it—?

JERZY: Make it flow.

(ISABEL, out:)

ISABEL: Jerzy was suspicious of assistants, they had a habit of suing him for credit. He asked me to work with him, and I was honored.

JERZY: Let's keep moving. A brief description of the woman—

ISABEL: Before we started, I told him I was pregnant.

JERZY: Brown hair, early twenties.

ISABEL: That he was the father.

JERZY: Attractive.

ISABEL: At my age, what are the chances? It was a miracle, *our* miracle. And after that…we didn't really discuss it.

JERZY: Watchful.

ISABEL: He didn't want to. I didn't bring it up.

JERZY: Unsure of herself, but in a way that's, er…

ISABEL: *(To* JERZY*)* Endearing?

JERZY: Endearing. Yes.

(ISABEL *goes back to typing—)*

(*Lights change to include* GEORGIA *seated at her desk.)*

JERZY: I walk into the office, she recognizes me.

GEORGIA: Mister Lesnewski!

JERZY: Her name is…Jean.

GEORGIA: I'm Georgia.

JERZY: Jean is at her desk…

(*Lights out on* ISABEL.)

GEORGIA: We met a few weeks ago.

JERZY: Oh yes!

(GEORGIA and JERZY shake hands, and he doesn't let go.

JERZY: I was with Paul and—

GEORGIA: I brought you a sandwich. Which isn't my job.

JERZY: I hope I didn't—

GEORGIA: No, I mean…I wanted to. I was getting one for myself anyway. I just meant, if I *had* to do it, it wouldn't have been much of a gesture, so…

(GEORGIA *trails off, hating herself.* JERZY *lets go of her hand.*)

JERZY: I'm looking for Arthur Bausley. I went to his office, they sent me here.

GEORGIA: Is this about the article? Conflicting dates…?

JERZY: *(Suspicious)* Yes…

GEORGIA: I've been working with Arthur. Checking facts. Which actually *is* my job.

JERZY: Ah. So you have a list of the "inconsistencies"?

GEORGIA: Arthur will want to be the one who…

JERZY: *(Holds a hand out)* Please.

(GEORGIA *hesitates, then hands* JERZY *a page. She waits nervously while he reads.*)

JERZY: "When was he separated from his parents?" The only one who can tell you that is me. You have to take my word.

GEORGIA: Except in your biography—

JERZY: The bio is wrong. These dates are right. Eh? I make your job easy.

GEORGIA: I guess.

(JERZY *looks at* GEORGIA *a moment.*)

JERZY: You're very beautiful. *(Pause)* So, we're done here?

GEORGIA: I…those are the only questions we…

JERZY: I won't bother you further. *(He starts out.)*

GEORGIA: Actually—Arthur should be back in a minute. If you don't mind…

JERZY: No...

(JERZY *takes a seat. A pause*)

GEORGIA: It's great to...really meet you. I've been thinking about you and your writing...

JERZY: You've been thinking about *me*?

GEORGIA: Well, I don't know you. The book...

JERZY: *(Pointing)* Is that your copy?

GEORGIA: Yes.

JERZY: Would you like me to sign it?

GEORGIA: I—

JERZY: Don't answer that. Sometimes I catch a glimpse of my ego, like the shadow of some huge, flapping—

GEORGIA: *(Holding book)* I'd appreciate it.

JERZY: Pen?

(GEORGIA *hands* JERZY *the book and a pen.*)

JERZY: *(Writing)* "Dear...?"

GEORGIA: Georgia.

JERZY: "—Georgia. I will never forget our time together. These last years have been one long... sexual...whirlwind. Love, Jerzy."

(JERZY *hands it back.*)

GEORGIA: That will confuse the biographers.

JERZY: Mine or yours?

GEORGIA: I don't think anyone's going to write about me. I'm happier spying on other people.

JERZY: Spying—

GEORGIA: Well I research. People with extraordinary lives. In your case...what you went through in the war, and in this country. Coming here with nothing and now you're famous—

JERZY: Not so extraordinary. Anyone can do this if they Exploit the Moment.

(GEORGIA *waits for him to explain.* JERZY's *chair is on coasters; he shoves off and coasts over to her.*)

JERZY: Always, even as a child, I felt an obligation to control each second as a dramatic unit. You understand? To analyze every situation as honestly as possible and then build on it.

GEORGIA: For example…

(JERZY *considers.*)

JERZY: You and I are waiting. We don't know each other. You're worried about my "inconsistencies", maybe you're a threat. But I find you attractive. I launch into a pretentious, semi-intellectual rant which is meant to impress you. Maybe you find it flattering, maybe you're suspicious. What do I want? Is it something you want to give?

GEORGIA: So we…boil it down to…

JERZY: Usually it's instinctive. But for the purpose of discussion, this moment is about…

GEORGIA: *(Beat)* Curiosity.

JERZY: Ah!

GEORGIA: I just mean, I've been reading your book, so—

JERZY: We have an obligation to curiosity. To surrender to it. Drown in it. And one course of action which comes to mind…

GEORGIA: Yes?

(*The phone rings.* GEORGIA *and* JERZY *both laugh.*)

GEORGIA: Probably Arthur.

(JERZY *leans back, and* GEORGIA *has to reach around him to answer it.*)

GEORGIA: Georgia speaking. What? No, she's already left. *(Makes a note)* Alright.

(JERZY is holding the cradle of the phone; perhaps it's in his lap. GEORGIA pauses before hanging up.)

GEORGIA: You were saying?

JERZY: *(Cavalier)* You get the idea.

GEORGIA: What if the moment already *is* what it is? Why do you want to make it more?

JERZY: To compensate for my own inadequacy.

GEORGIA: *What* inadequacy?

JERZY: I don't want to burden you...

GEORGIA: No, go ahead.

(JERZY takes a deep breath.)

JERZY: When I was young, I was attacked by a group of children. There was a little girl... You know this from my book.

(GEORGIA nods.)

JERZY: What you don't know is...they left me damaged. *(Then)* They took a stick. And did things... *(Then)* ...to my penis.

GEORGIA: Oh...!

(A beat)

JERZY: Have I upset you?

GEORGIA: I'm... That's very...

JERZY: You feel repulsed?

GEORGIA: Not at all.

JERZY: *(With a twinkle)* Curious?

GEORGIA: Is it *true*?

JERZY: *(Getting up)* What do you mean, "is it true"—? *(Quickly)* Come have a drink with me.

GEORGIA: When?

JERZY: Now.

GEORGIA: I have to work. Otherwise I…I'd love to, but—

JERZY: Can I use your phone? *(Dials a number)* Hello, Paul? Jerzy. I'm working with a research assistant of yours, Georgia…?

GEORGIA: Fischer.

JERZY: *(Into phone)* Georgia Fischer. Mind if I borrow her for awhile? I'll return her in roughly the same condition. Thanks. *(Hangs up)* Get your coat.

GEORGIA: We're going out.

JERZY: Yes.

GEORGIA: Because…we have an obligation to…

JERZY: Exactly.

(Light on GEORGIA.)

GEORGIA: When he wrote about me he used the name Jean. Outside of that he didn't change much. The first night we had dinner then went to his apartment. And his penis was fine so…I guess it was a joke. Or something.

Seven

(Lights up on ARTHUR, MRS GRUSZKA and RYSIEK in RYSIEK's cramped kitchen. MRS GRUSZKA keeps her distance, lingering in the background.)

ARTHUR: In front of everyone?

RYSIEK: The people looking, he don't care.

ARTHUR: He slapped the glass while you were telling a story—

RYSIEK: Yes.

ARTHUR: Which he didn't want them to hear?

RYSIEK: Yes.

ARTHUR: What was the story?

(RYSIEK *hesitates.*)

RYSIEK: A guy is making movie for Jerzy. One of these guys. He say this book—so good, okay? Boy comes to village, a girl pointing at him. Other boys come out, they fight…

ARTHUR: They rape him.

RYSIEK: Good movie, okay. What I say is not so good.

ARTHUR: Were you there when it happened?

RYSIEK: In Krasnystaw…

ARTHUR: But were you there when—specifically, when the boys…

RYSIEK: They were not doing a rape. They pull his pants to see. Check him. If he was cut.

ARTHUR: Cut?

RYSIEK: Jewish.

ARTHUR: Circumsized.

RYSIEK: I tell them stop, they stop.

ARTHUR: That's it?

RYSIEK: Book is better, eh? Cause I'm not in it.

(ARTHUR *jots a note.*)

ARTHUR: They thought he *looked* Jewish, is that why they—?

RYSIEK: My cousin, Kasia. In the book.

ARTHUR: The little girl…

MRS GRUSZKA: *Kasia.*

(RYSIEK *is forced to acknowledge* MRS GRUSZKA.)

RYSIEK: Osucha Gruszka, my aunt. Kasia's mother.

MRS GRUSZKA: *Powiedz. Powiedz mu o Lesnewskim. (To* ARTHUR) *Morderca.*

ARTHUR: What is she—?

RYSIEK: *(Dismissive)* I don't know.

MRS GRUSZKA: *Morderca.*

RYSIEK: *Chcialbym rozmawiac z nim osobiscie.*

MRS GRUSZKA: *Enh?*

RYSIEK: *Hoch, hoch.*

(MRS GRUSZKA *exits.*)

ARTHUR: What does "*morderca*" mean?

RYSIEK: I tell what happened.

ARTHUR: She kept—

RYSIEK: I tell you. *(Then)* Kasia and Jerzy are same age, he likes her. Looking at her, giving things, okay, flowers and things and—he tell her, "shh, I am a Jew." Kasia is only ten so…she tell brother. Mother, father, me. Everyone.

ARTHUR: Told everyone he was Jewish.

RYSIEK: The boys try to see…

ARTHUR: —if he was circumsized. And you stopped them.

RYSIEK: Then Jerzy tell Kasia it's a joke. He's not a Jew, of course not a Jew. She is stupid she believe. So then they never talk.

ARTHUR: Was Jerzy already in Krasnystaw? *(Off* RYSIEK) In the book, the first time the boy walks into the village he gets attacked. You're saying Jerzy brought Kasia flowers, so he was already there.

RYSIEK: He was, yeah…

ARTHUR: Where was he living?

RYSIEK: With his parents. *(Then)* I don't understand.

*(*ARTHUR *is staring at* RYSIEK.*)*

ARTHUR: He was living with his parents?

RYSIEK: Yeah.

ARTHUR: In Krasnystaw.

RYSIEK: After the war, they move to Lodz…

ARTHUR: Wait. Wait. *(Then)* Why has no one said this?

RYSIEK: It's not secret. People in my village—

ARTHUR: The whole premise of the book. The boy is alone, no parents.

RYSIEK: But the book is—it's a book. Yes?

Eight

(Light on ISABEL*)*

ISABEL: I bought a crib with high ratings for safety and a European stroller. It started to sink in how different, how insane life will be with a baby. You know newborns can cry for up to four hours a day? I read that. It said when a baby is hungry their cry is short and low-pitched, when they're in pain they shriek and when they're angry they wail. I thought, at if I can't tell the difference between a shriek and a wail? But my child will be more articulate. *(Then)* I admitted I'm pregnant to my friend with cancer. I was afraid I'd be rubbing her nose in my happiness, and she did tear up. Then she smiled and said: what a wonderful thing for us to look forward to! I said yes. We'll go through it together. She seemed to like that.

Nine

(Lights up on JERZY *and* GEORGIA *in his apartment.)*

JERZY: Come on, I'm restless.

GEORGIA: I don't even know what a sex club is.

JERZY: A club where people have sex.

GEORGIA: Where *we* have sex?

JERZY: We can watch.

GEORGIA: Yeah, I don't think I'm up for that tonight. *(Then)* You do this a lot?

JERZY: Sure.

GEORGIA: What's wrong?

JERZY: I told you, I'm restless. *(Then)* Your friend Arthur called.

GEORGIA: Yeah?

JERZY: He's writing another fucking article. Getting statements from everyone who wants me wiped out, which fortunately for him is half of New York and all of Poland. I'm going through this shit with the Guild and he calls—

GEORGIA: When was this?

JERZY: Monday.

GEORGIA: Why didn't you tell me then? I'm on your side. You might try letting go around me, be yourself instead of—

JERZY: Tell me how I should act in order to "be myself".

GEORGIA: Jerzy.

JERZY: How you are with your mother is different from how you are with me. To say: now! Now we will be ourselves.

GEORGIA: How do you act around your mother?

JERZY: She's dead, thank you—

GEORGIA: Your father?

JERZY: It's not the point.

GEORGIA: *(Overlapping)* When you first saw your father after being separated all those years, were you angry? I know he was trying to save you—

JERZY: This "opening up" is bullshit. The only time we drop our guard is when we're surprised, in pain or having sex. That's it.

GEORGIA: I don't. Not during sex.

JERZY: Then we're not having good sex. When someone says "I feel naked," they refer to vulnerability. Nobody thinks about how they look while they're having an orgasm. If they did, they wouldn't have one. *(Then)* What do you fantasize about?

GEORGIA: You're changing the subject.

JERZY: I'm not, not at all. Pick a fantasy you wouldn't want anyone to know…tell it to me.

(A beat)

GEORGIA: There's one that… You were talking about the sex club, so I… But it never happened.

JERZY: Of course not. *(Then)* Come on…

GEORGIA: I'm working at a clothing store watching for shoplifters. Sitting behind a one-way mirror that looks in on a changing room. And the customers don't realize they're being watched. A man comes in.

JERZY: Mm.

GEORGIA: Starts to get undressed. Slowly. Not just his shirt or pants, he totally strips down. I notice he didn't bring any clothes to try on. Then he turns to the mirror and he has an erection. I sit looking at him while he… touches himself. Then he looks into my eyes. And I realize, he could see me the whole time. *(Pause)* There are different endings. That's the basic…

JERZY: You should get undressed.

GEORGIA: Tell *me* one.

JERZY: Later, I think now you should—

GEORGIA: We were having a conversation, I don't want to—

JERZY: It's about being vulnerable.

(With clinical indifference, GEORGIA *removes her clothes and faces* JERZY.)

GEORGIA: How's that? Am I vulnerable?

JERZY: No, now you're making a point. Now it's a lecture.

*(*GEORGIA *covers herself with a blanket from the couch.)*

JERZY: I need to get out. I'm going out, you can come if you like.

(As JERZY *starts off—)*

GEORGIA:Here. *(She takes a blue notebook out of her bag.)* My diary. *(Hands it over)* I don't edit anything. Crazy thoughts, spiteful thoughts. Sex stuff. Parts about us you may not like—

JERZY: What do you want from me? You want something. I can't make a trade.

GEORGIA: No trade. No…strings.

*(*JERZY *flips open the diary.)*

GEORGIA:Now I feel naked. *(Then)* This is between us…

(Lights change to reveal ISABEL, *typing.)*

ISABEL: This is…between…us.

JERZY: Whatever you want.

ISABEL: *(Typing)* Whatever…you…want.

JERZY: *(To* ISABEL*)* Read it back?

ISABEL: *(Flat)* No trade no strings. Now I feel naked.
This is between us. Whatever you want.

(Lights out on GEORGIA. JERZY *crosses to* ISABEL, *still
holding the blue notebook. He reads a moment over her
shoulder.)*

JERZY: Fine.

Ten

*(*ARTHUR *and* WITOLD TWAROG *in a dressing room.*
WITOLD *is sewing a hat, part of a period costume. Opera
music plays faintly in the background.)*

WITOLD: A man tells us he was on the bus, an old
woman spilled coffee on his leg. A few nights later I
hear Jerzy tell the story, now apparently he was there,
he can describe in *detail* the pain on the man's face.
Next Jerzy says it happened to *him.* Ah!, agony, coffee
on his thigh, perfume as he leans on the beautiful
woman—who now of course is beautiful.

ARTHUR: When was this?

WITOLD: I was nineteen. Studying design in Lodz. For
Jerzy it was photography, he wasn't a writer then.

ARTHUR: You both grew up during the war. Ever
compare notes?

(Off WITOLD*)*

ARTHUR: You did.

WITOLD: My accounts were not as vivid as his.

ARTHUR: When you read *Vantage Point*, are those the
stories he was telling in Lodz? Or did they change.

(A YOUNG MAN *hurries in wearing torn pants and a
muddy shirt, his face smeared with dirt.)*

WITOLD: Ah yes— *(To* ARTHUR*)* Peasants rise up in the third act.

*(*WITOLD *looks the* YOUNG MAN *over.)*

ARTHUR: There's a Polish journalist who interviewed people Jerzy knew during the war and there are differing—

WITOLD: The journalist. Mierowiecka, yes? Raging anti-Semite. *(To the* YOUNG MAN*)* More on the neck.

(The YOUNG MAN *exits.* WITOLD *watches him go with some interest.)*

ARTHUR: What I'm getting at—

WITOLD: I'm starting to wonder.

ARTHUR: Jerzy never wandered through Poland alone, he was living with his parents.

(Off WITOLD*)*

ARTHUR: You've heard that.

WITOLD: Maybe I miss the point.

ARTHUR: Since you *were* alone as a boy, I'm wondering if Jerzy borrowed his stories from you.

(A beat)

WITOLD: *(Lightly)* He can have my stories. I'm not using them.

ARTHUR: Well. That's generous, but people should know if—

WITOLD: Jerzy and I did not live in a world of truth. Anybody who survived under German occupation would have to accept that certain lies are necessary for survival. Anybody who lived in the Polish reality of Stalin would very early understand it's all great hypocrisy and lies. *(He breaks the thread with his teeth and puts on the hat.)* How's it look?

ARTHUR: Good.

(WITOLD *checks himself in the mirror.*)

WITOLD: Hardly. But thank you all the same.

Eleven

(*Light on the actor playing* JERZY, *as we hear the recorded voice of* KASIA [*an 8 year-old girl with no accent*]. *Eventually the actor playing* JERZY *speaks along with the girl, speaking as* KASIA, *exactly matching phrases.* [*There might be a photo of* KASIA *on an overhead.*])

KASIA: I lost Osucha's bracelet. I wanted to wear it and she said no but I can wear it when I'm older maybe, when I have a wedding dress. But I was looking and… so I brought it outside to look at it? And Zoja was chasing me and then I lost it. Even though I looked for probably two hours. And this boy Jerzy is next door and he was watching, even though I didn't want him to watch me. He asked how come I was crying and I didn't tell him because I said it wasn't any of his business.

(*Light on* GEORGIA.)

GEORGIA: I needed to fall asleep. I thought, maybe if I read something screamingly boring. So I got out of bed, Jerzy mumbled something but didn't wake up, and I went into his study. Spent twenty minutes reading about pre-war Poland, then a collection of untranslated Czech poetry. I don't speak Czech so that *was* boring. I tried a hardcover, 1965 New York City census report… and in retrospect, I know why he had it. It was the book he thought no one would read.

KASIA: Jerzy said if I tell him a secret, he'll tell me one. If I was touching his face. You touch someone's face, you know it's true, that's what Zoja says. I told him I lost Osucha's bracelet. Now tell me something:

GEORGIA: An old photo fell out of the book.

(GEORGIA *holds up an old, yellowed photograph, gazing at it. [There could be a still photo on an overhead: a neatly dressed young boy posing with his mother. She has a hand on his shoulder as he gazes directly at the camera, emboldened by her presence.]*)

GEORGIA: It was a young boy with his mother. The woman had her hand on the boy's shoulder, both of them staring into the camera. There was a date on the back. "March 3rd, 1944." *(Then)* Then I realized who it was. But at that age, Jerzy with his mother? It didn't make sense. And then it did. *(She goes to* JERZY, *touches his face.)* I wanted to wake him. Say shhh, you're safe with me…

JERZY: He's a Jew. And promise not to tell, now. Promise, promise. Promise, promise, promise.

GEORGIA: Instead I put my arms around him. And closed my eyes.

Twelve

(ARTHUR's *office. He waits for* GEORGIA *to finish reading some typed notes.*)

GEORGIA: *(Finally)* Okay.

ARTHUR: Okay? He was with his parents, "okay". The lone Jewish boy.

GEORGIA: If you say so.

(ARTHUR *studies* GEORGIA *a moment.*)

ARTHUR: You already knew.

GEORGIA: No and I'm not convinced what you're—

ARTHUR: He told you. Right? Except he wouldn't tell you. So you figured it out.

GEORGIA: Is this how you get material? Accusations, assumptions.

ARTHUR: Not only can I prove Jerzy lied, I know *why*. *(More pages)* He's ashamed.

GEORGIA: Of what?

ARTHUR: Jerzy's father was an informant for the Russians.

GEORGIA: Arthur.

ARTHUR: Krasnystaw was overrun by the Russians after the war. To guarantee the safety of his own family, Jerzy's father gave the soldiers names of villagers who posed a threat. Nine men were dragged out of their homes and shot. *(Hands her pages)* Polish journalist named Mierowiecka.

(GEORGIA looks it over.)

ARTHUR: If your father pulled something like that, wouldn't you be tempted to maybe—skim over that part...

GEORGIA: You consider the motives and politics of this journalist—

ARTHUR: I found someone who was there.

GEORGIA: Who?

(ARTHUR doesn't answer, basking in her frustration.)

GEORGIA: Jerzy's father has nothing to do with him or his writing.

ARTHUR: I disagree.

GEORGIA: Even if he did lie. That makes it less of a book?

ARTHUR: Yes!

GEORGIA: You said he was one of the greatest writers of the century. That you identified with him as an outsider, that he provoked the reader by—

ARTHUR: Who do we side with here? The guy who wants answers or the guy who invents Holocaust stories?

GEORGIA: You're trashing his career to score a front-page column.

(ARTHUR *picks up a cardboard box and sets it on his desk.*)

ARTHUR: What's that?

GEORGIA: I don't know. Your fan mail.

ARTHUR: It's what you put your stuff in when they force you to resign.

(Off her)

ARTHUR: Ferryman asked what I had on Jerzy. I showed him and he said dogs would grow wings before he'd print it. I told him if *he* wasn't interested, the Village Voice would be. Ergo, cardboard box.

GEORGIA: You're quitting out of spite.

ARTHUR: Is that it? Am I a resentful person or do I maybe believe this is important?

GEORGIA: You're a martyr—

ARTHUR: We think perception is subjective, there's no such thing as truth. Of course there is. Creativity isn't a gift, it's a privilege. There are conditions. Our country fights a war in Quang Tri, half-way around the world. When we open the morning paper, that's an act of faith.

(GEORGIA *turns to leave.*)

ARTHUR: Ferryman knows you slept with Jerzy.

GEORGIA: *(Beat)* How?

ARTHUR: Cause I told him.

GEORGIA: What did he say?

ARTHUR: He's letting you go. *(Then)* Look, I'm leaving too—

GEORGIA: It's a little different—

ARTHUR: Work with me at the *Voice*. You've been a fact-checker for how long? I could get you a byline.

GEORGIA: On what?

ARTHUR: You know Jerzy better than anyone, if we wrote this together—wait, hear me out. It would be an unbiased—

GEORGIA: I feel sorry for you.

ARTHUR: *(Reaching out)* I'm saying we—

(GEORGIA *pulls violently away, stares at* ARTHUR. *Exits)*

Thirteen

(JERZY *and the arbiters for the Authors Guild,* SORVILLO *and* KERRY.*)*

JERZY: What *translation?*

SORVILLO: We have evidence that—

(JERZY *gets up as if to leave.)*

JERZY: I can't come here every day for this, I don't have time. Do you believe Duffy's stupid claim or not?

KERRY: Mister Duffy asserts you were having difficulty phrasing your ideas in English. That his contributions were stylistic—

JERZY: I know what he *asserts*.

KERRY: He believes you initially wrote in Polish and hired someone to translate. That he would then work on turning these rough translations into a more graceful form of prose.

JERZY: *(Sits)* I would never write in Polish.

SORVILLO: Why not?

JERZY: Memories from that time are painful. By using a new language, I was able to access—

SORVILLO: A woman named Marianna Piekarski says she responded to an ad of yours in the *Saturday Review* seeking a translator. That she refused because you told her she'd be paid but not get credit for her work. *(Then)* I spoke to Marianna myself—

JERZY: Why are you attacking me?

KERRY: What?

JERZY: This whole process…I thought I could trust the Guild to conduct an investigation, but obviously…

SORVILLO: We're trying to—

JERZY: There is a reporter in the hallway. Outside this door. Why is that?

SORVILLO: I wasn't aware—

JERZY: The man is trying to slander me. Why was he allowed in the building?

KERRY: It's public property, we can't restrict—

JERZY: I pay dues for the Guild to *protect* me. If every author had to work so hard to defend what they write…! To argue about some woman who didn't want a job no one needed her to do.

KERRY: *(To SORVILLO)* Read the ad.

SORVILLO: *(Clears his throat, then reads)* "Translator wanted, Polish to English, for full-length fiction to be translated in short time."

KERRY: We've confirmed this was placed by a "J. Lesnewski", one year before you submitted your manuscript.

(A beat)

JERZY: *(Calmly)* Next time we meet I'd like to bring someone.

SORVILLO: An attorney?

JERZY: A scientist. He studies Holocaust survivors in situations of stress. This is an opportunity for him—

KERRY: Mister Lesnewski, did you place the ad?

JERZY: *(Pause)* I might have.

KERRY: Can you tell us why?

JERZY: At one point, I was considering a different book. The collected accounts of Polish children during the war. I may have thought I needed help with translation.

(A beat)

KERRY: Anything you'd like to add to that?

JERZY: No.

KERRY: If you could provide us with any notes you may have from this...other book.

JERZY: I'll see what I can find.

KERRY: Thank you for coming.

JERZY: You're...you're welcome.

(KERRY *and* SORVILLO *begin collecting their papers.* KERRY *reaches to turn off the tape recorder.)*

JERZY: Please—

(KERRY *looks up.)*

JERZY: Every word is mine. Not only the presence of the word but the reasons why.

KERRY: We've heard—

JERZY: Every manuscript, middle draft, final draft, every fucking galley. First page proof, second, third, hardcover and paperback editions. They were *all mine*.

KERRY: We'll take that into consideration.

(Lights change as the KERRY *and* SORVILLO *exit.* JERZY *sits as* ARTHUR *approaches.)*

JERZY: The vultures are circling.

ARTHUR: You don't return my calls.

JERZY: Why the fuck would I? *(Then)* What do you want?

ARTHUR: Another interview.

*(*JERZY *laughs.)*

JERZY: Write it yourself. Talk to Duffy…

ARTHUR: It's not about Duffy.

JERZY: Then to which bit of scandal will I be responding? My personal life, sex life—

ARTHUR: You wrote that you were alone during the war.

*(*JERZY *looks at* ARTHUR.*)*

ARTHUR: I'm sure Georgia told you…

JERZY: *(Lightly)* Told me?

ARTHUR: My article…

JERZY: *(Lightly)* No I don't think she did. Though I'm accused of so many absurdities lately—it's like recalling a specific penguin at the zoo.

ARTHUR: If you're available next—

JERZY: What do you mean, "I'm sure Georgia told you." You discuss it with her? *(Then)* You approach a friend of mine…

ARTHUR: We spoke about—

JERZY: Behind my back you go to—

ARTHUR: Jerzy. *(Then)* She already knew.

Fourteen

(Light on GEORGIA*)*

GEORGIA: It wasn't like I was waiting for Jerzy to leave so I could go through his stuff... It's just, he would leave and...I'd go through his stuff— My point is, I wasn't feeling suspicious. We'd gotten closer since I gave him my diary, and finding his photo—it was like finding a window, I wanted to pry it open. Then I came across his manuscript, I figured he'd ask me to read it soon, anyway. Flipping through it, I thought, wow, he got this dialogue from me. This part, too... Then it hit me. I tore the place apart looking for my diary, but couldn't find it. I left, and freaked out for three days before I called.

(Lights change; GEORGIA *is with* JERZY *and* ISABEL *in his living room.)*

GEORGIA: You found it *useful*?

ISABEL: If it was me, I'd be honored—

GEORGIA: So let him have your journal.

ISABEL: He doesn't want mine.

JERZY: I meant it as an homage. To you, to us. There's an honesty to it.

GEORGIA: Of course there is, it's a fucking diary! You don't lie in your diary. I mean some of us don't.

ISABEL: Georgia—

GEORGIA: Oh look, it's honesty! Must be something *useful* we can do with it...

JERZY: You go though my things too, eh? And think I don't notice. At least I'm making art, not indulging in gossip.

(A beat)

GEORGIA: What does *that* mean?

JERZY: What you discuss with Arthur. Sharing theories.

ISABEL: I'm sure you didn't mean any harm, but sweetheart…

GEORGIA: I would never—

JERZY: It's wonderful. Curiosity. An extension of our affection. To explore as a journalist…

GEORGIA: I didn't tell Arthur anything. *(Beat)* If you believe I would—

JERZY: Believe *what?!* As opposed to…? Resting my head in your lap, I am safe from *everything?* "Don't be *defensive,* Jerzy. Give yourself to me, I will go through your papers, we will be *so close!!*" *(He closes his eyes a moment.)* What do you think of it so far, this article of Arthur's? You did read it?

*(*GEORGIA *turns to* ISABEL.*)*

GEORGIA: Would it be alright if… Could we have a minute alone?

*(*ISABEL *glares at* GEORGIA, *then goes into the next room.)*

GEORGIA: It doesn't sound right, to say I went through your stuff because I care about you but… *(Then)* I found a picture. You and your mother. There's a date on the back.

JERZY: So?

GEORGIA: I want to know you, I'm starting to feel—

JERZY: Explain this. A date on the back, it means…?

GEORGIA: Your mother was with you.

(A pause)

JERZY: You drew this conclusion, but didn't confront me.

GEORGIA: I was hoping you'd tell me yourself.

JERZY: Right. I'll tell you. *(Then)* After the war. When I was fourteen. I was reunited with my parents—

GEORGIA: You were with them the whole—

JERZY: *Shut up!! Shut up!!* ...I am telling you. *(Calmly)* I was reunited with my parents. And we moved into a furnished house. The Soviets gave my father the house of some German family. But these people didn't move out, they vanished. We *replaced* them. There was milk in the ice box. A stuffed donkey, I played with it like it was always mine. And there were pictures of strangers on the walls. For days until my mother took them down. One of them, in my room...a photo of a boy and his mother.

GEORGIA: Your name is on the back—

JERZY: I think now, it's very sad. For a boy to make this up.

GEORGIA: No...

JERZY: I needed a memory of my mother from the years I lost. That boy...I stole his memory.

GEORGIA: It's you in the picture.

JERZY: It's not. I'll show you. *(He heads for the desk.)*

GEORGIA: I have it. With me. *(Then)* When I couldn't find my diary...I was angry, I...

JERZY: Let me see.

*(*GEORGIA *hands it to* JERZY.*)*

JERZY: That is not my mother. It looks nothing like her.

GEORGIA: Well I've never seen your—

JERZY: And that is not me.

GEORGIA: It is! Those are your eyes.

JERZY: This picture is…it's a toy. It means nothing. *(He rips it in two.)*

GEORGIA: Oh my God! *(Then)* I'm so sorry…

JERZY: A boy I never knew. He is not part of my life.

GEORGIA: I did this…I did this.

(JERZY takes a pack of matches from a drawer and lights one.)

GEORGIA: No! No, please…

(JERZY sets the photo on fire and drops it onto a plate to finish burning.)

JERZY: Why are you upset? There's no reason. Look at me. I'm not upset.

(Cautiously, ISABEL steps into the room.)

JERZY: I'll be right back.

(JERZY moves past ISABEL and exits.)

ISABEL: All of us around here, we're so *dramatic*. *(Then)* Was he burning something?

GEORGIA: *(Crying)* Oh my God…

(ISABEL goes over and gently strokes GEORGIA's hair.)

ISABEL: Don't be so hard on yourself. I know what you want. To feel like you share something with him. And you do. But…maybe not in the way you were hoping. If he says it's not him in the photo—

GEORGIA: You were listening.

ISABEL: You were yelling.

(GEORGIA pulls away.)

ISABEL: It would never occur to me, to question what he says. Why would I?

GEORGIA: It was his picture, probably the only one he saved. You'd know that if you weren't lost in your own...bitter, jealous...

ISABEL: *(Coolly)* Surprising as it may seem, I don't feel I have to compete with a dilettante, twenty-six year-old Sarah Lawrence Lit Grad. I've *procured* girls for him and watched them go at it on my living room rug while I ate cheese and crackers. If you had the slightest comprehension of what Jerzy and I share...

GEORGIA: You sleep with him?

ISABEL: I don't need to. Our relationship isn't based on physical gratification. It goes deeper.

GEORGIA: Oh *please*—

ISABEL: In fact, I'm...

GEORGIA: *(Pause)* You're what?

(A beat)

ISABEL: Don't be angry with him. He cares about you. He's just frightened.

(JERZY returns with a sheaf of copied pages.)

JERZY: Isabel and I made this because we knew you'd want it. To have while I'm working.

(JERZY hands GEORGIA the sheaf.)

GEORGIA: A photocopy...

JERZY: Of your diary.

GEORGIA: *(Pause)* There are sections blacked out.

JERZY: Only a few parts. The more...susceptible parts.

GEORGIA: Oh. *(Then)* Well then. Thank you.

Fifteen

(HARRY *and* JERZY *in* HARRY's *office.*)

HARRY: They're not the only producers in Hollywood. At some point this crap with the Guild blows over—

JERZY: They wanted to make the movie, now they don't. You know why?

HARRY: Jerzy, I have a conference in three minutes.

JERZY: They smell fear. This offensive odor of despair, it's killing me.

HARRY: If you'd called before—

JERZY: I know how we get back on top. Eh?

(JERZY *opens the door and leans into the hallway.*)

HARRY: I don't have time…

JERZY: Come in!

(JERZY'S FATHER *enters.*)

JERZY: Harry. My father.

HARRY: You're kidding.

JERZY: This is Harry, my agent.

JERZY'S FATHER: Hello.

HARRY: It's…a pleasure. I've heard a lot about you…

(JERZY *puts his arm around his father.*)

JERZY: He can do interviews!

HARRY: What?

JERZY: He'll talk about everything. Our separation…

HARRY: Maybe if we wait—

JERZY: We have to do it before they run Arthur's article. You contact Paul, tell him to send someone over. He should do a feature, take pictures…

HARRY: I don't know.

JERZY: Why not?

HARRY: Paul's gonna want to wait for the *Voice* article before he goes out on a limb.

JERZY: What limb! This is my father!

HARRY: Yeah, but… *(Glances at his watch)* Jerzy. I have to check in down the hall.

JERZY: I'll call him myself. *(Picks up the phone)* Paul's number, remind me…

HARRY: My friend, you need to hang tough. There's a lot going on. The Guild, this thing with Isabel, the Voice article. If we keep calm—

JERZY: Thing with Isabel?

HARRY: *(Pause)* She didn't tell you?

JERZY: Of course she told *me*…

(HARRY watches JERZY a moment.)

HARRY: Give me a minute.

(HARRY exits. JERZY hangs up the phone.)

JERZY'S FATHER: *Dlaczego nie zapytal?*

JERZY: *Bo wroci.*

JERZY'S FATHER: *Posadz go tutaj, ja mu powiem. Ty nie jestes z nami.*

JERZY: Mm.

(A beat)

JERZY'S FATHER: You were not with us. *(Then)* I say to him: he was not with us—

JERZY: *(Annoyed)* Right. Of course.

JERZY'S FATHER: *(Pause)* I say to him—

JERZY: Please, will you…

(JERZY *gets his father up.*)

JERZY: Wait for me in the hall. (*Points*) In that chair. Eh?

JERZY'S FATHER: *Kiedy wroci, posadz go tu tai, ja mu
powiem—*

JERZY: *Prosze.*

(JERZY'S FATHER *exits.* JERZY *goes to* HARRY's *desk, flips
through a rolodex and gets the number he wants. He starts
to dial—then cries out and slams the phone down. He takes a
few steps and drops into an armchair, shaking.*)

(HARRY *enters.*)

HARRY: I have a reprieve.

(JERZY *turns away, managing a casual tone.*)

JERZY: Good.

HARRY: First. About Isabel…

JERZY: I can't understand her. Telling everyone.

HARRY: That's her right, isn't it?

JERZY: It's… No! It is not. When she was first pregnant,
we had a discussion—

HARRY: Pregnant? (*Pause*) Is that what she said? That
she's pregnant?

JERZY: It's getting obvious. Her belly.

HARRY: Jerzy.

JERZY: What?

HARRY: The doctor I referred her to, he's my brother-
in-law. Anything she told you about being pregnant,
that's just… It's a nice fantasy.

JERZY: I don't think so.

HARRY: Isabel has stomach cancer. That's why her
belly… She's sick.

(*A beat*)

JERZY: She bought a crib. Little toys...

HARRY: She's creative, right? That's what we love about her.

(Light on ISABEL*)*

ISABEL: The weather was gorgeous. I walked the whole way to Jerzy's, people were out. There's a tree on seventy-second street that must be, I don't know how old, I had my coffee looking up through the branches. You could see every vein in the leaves. I thought, when I was a girl I might've walked past this tree without seeing it. Now it's huge. *(Then)* I went up to Jerzy's. He seemed distracted, probably the business with the Guild, and we weren't getting a lot of work done. Then out of the blue he—

*(*JERZY *gives* ISABEL *a gentle kiss on the cheek.)*

ISABEL: We sat there. Sunlight spilling in through the windows. It was nice.

Sixteen

(Light on GEORGIA *as she addresses* JERZY *in his dimly lit apartment.)*

GEORGIA: Sorry to barge in. Did you hear me outside? You don't answer the phone—I mean, there's no law that says you have to but...I was worried. It doesn't smell good in here, isn't Elena coming? You didn't fire her, did you? *(Then)* Jerzy. Is this about the article?

(Lights up on ARTHUR, MRS GRUSZKA *and* RYSIEK *in a conference room.)*

ARTHUR: *(To* JERZY*)* You know Rysiek. His aunt, Osucha Gruszka. You might remember her from Krasnystaw—or at least, she remembers you. They're going to help us form an account of certain events, iron out discrepancies. If you want to take a moment, get reacquainted?

GEORGIA: Can we talk about it? Jerzy, please?

ARTHUR: Then let's get started.

(Light out on GEORGIA *as—)*

*(*JERZY *[now in the conference room] bursts into a feverish rant, by turns impassioned and exhausted, drained.)*

JERZY: The first woman I slept with had breasts like couch pillows. Eh? Like sandbags! When we describe a memory, we simplify to distill the essence of what we felt. And for children the grasp of details is not so good, emotions are overwhelming, fear becomes hallucination—

ARTHUR: When you were in Krasnytaw during the war. You lived in a thatched house with two rooms, on the edge of a field. And you lived with your parents. Is that right?

JERZY: Is what right?

ARTHUR: What I described. You were living with your parents.

JERZY: Can't picture it.

ARTHUR: *(*MRS GRUSZKA *and* RYSIEK*)* But that's what they remember. I spoke with each of them separately, they describe you with your parents, right through to the end of the war. Are they lying?

JERZY: Last year I drove my car into a wall. Smashed both knee caps.

ARTHUR: Jerzy—

JERZY: The police gave me a form to describe the event. I said well, a blur of color, a car coming I think right at me, horns and maybe I hear screaming. Someone throws a wall of bricks in my face, my blood splatters

across the windshield. I look down, it's not my blood,
I left a tomato juice on the dashboard. Then I imagine
I'm with a friend drinking tomato juice. In his kitchen,
under a sunlight. Pleasant. And still the car horn is
going, my legs are in the steering wheel...I say to the
police, is *this* what you want?

(ARTHUR *jumps in—*)

ARTHUR: From seven to fourteen, you have no
recollection of being with your parents?

JERZY: You read my book.

ARTHUR: You wrote what you remember?

JERZY: Yes, or...I remember what I wrote.

ARTHUR: That's different.

JERZY: There were boys playing a game by the pond,
holding each other's heads under water til they were
almost unconscious. Ridiculous, eh? And men coming
back from the field. Carrying lanterns. Pricks of light.
I thought, that would be nice. To carry a lantern with
those men.

ARTHUR: (*Off* MRS GRUSZKA *and* RYSIEK) You've heard
their account. Is it possible something happened when
you were a kid, made you want to excise your parents
from the story? Erase them—

JERZY: (*Snaps*) *Sounds* good, doesn't it. The psychology.
Fascinating.

ARTHUR: (*Pressing*) I got a call from a man in
Krasnystaw, says he has a copy of your parent's lease.
So people aren't going to ask *did* Jerzy lie, they're
gonna ask *why*.

RYSIEK: Remember Kasia? You play together and--
talking and—

JERZY: No. No, I'm sorry. I want to help, I do...

(Frustrated, ARTHUR *leaps up and points to* MRS GRUSZKA.*)*

ARTHUR: You can sit across from this woman and say you were alone as a boy? When your father gave the names of nine men to Russian soldiers, and those men were murdered.

JERZY: What? *(Off* MRS GRUSZKA*)* She said this?

ARTHUR: Mrs Gruszka was held down while her husband was pulled from their living room, dragged outside and shot in the back of the head.

JERZY: You think my father had Mister Gruszka killed.

ARTHUR: To ensure *your* survival. *(Beat)* No one's gonna ask *did* Jerzy lie, they're gonna ask *why*.

*(*JERZY *strains, as if struggling to see into the dark.)*

JERZY: *(Beat)* I have…images of…

ARTHUR: Were you with your parents?

(A beat—and JERZY *relaxes. Focused, even transfixed.)*

JERZY: Yes.

*(*ARTHUR *bolts over to the tape recorder, makes sure it's running.)*

ARTHUR: You *were*. Living with your parents.

JERZY: My mother, father.

ARTHUR: The Gruszkas were your neighbors?

JERZY: I had a window looking into their yard. Rusted cart in the corner, stack of wood—

ARTHUR: The night Mister Gruszka was killed.

JERZY: During the summer. After dinner, sun is setting. I can picture it…I'm playing with a cloth doll my mother gave me. Making it dance. We hear the shot.

ARTHUR: You heard it.

JERZY: We jump. My father…I see him. Walking to the table. Sitting down. Repeating to himself: forgive me. Forgive me…

(RYSIEK *stands.*)

RYSIEK: Why do you say this?

ARTHUR: Rysiek—

RYSIEK: When my uncle was shot, your father was in Lodz.

JERZY: He was? *(He stares at* RYSIEK, *genuinely horrified.)* No, I—have a clear picture…

ARTHUR: Wait a minute—

RYSIEK: His father was not giving names to Russians.

ARTHUR: I'd like to hear—

RYSIEK: My uncle dies, his family lives. They are Jews. How is it they live, Osucha does not understand.

ARTHUR: You *think* his father was in Lodz but…you were young—

RYSIEK: *(Turns)* Osucha.

JERZY: So strange…

RYSIEK: *Kiedy wujek byl zastrzelony czy jego ojciec byl w Krasnystaw?*

MRS GRUSZKA: *Nie.*

RYSIEK: Lesnewski was not there.

MRS GRUSZKA: *Ja powinnam wydac go Szwaba.*

RYSIEK: What she say? She should have given them to Nazis.

(ARTHUR *stares at* MRS GRUSZKA. *Turns to* JERZY.)

ARTHUR: Why would you make that up? Why would you *ever* make that up? *(Turns off tape recorder)* It made *sense.*

(JERZY *looks to* RYSIEK.)

JERZY: Were there boys at the pond?

RYSIEK: We used to play there.

JERZY: And men with lanterns.

RYSIEK: Every night. *(Then)* You remember Kasia? You told her everything.

JERZY: That must have been nice.

Seventeen

(ARTHUR, *seated at a restaurant, looking startled as* HARRY *stands over him.)*

HARRY: *(Calmly)* Feel good about yourself?

ARTHUR: What?

HARRY: I asked, do you feel good about yourself.

(ARTHUR, *out:)*

ARTHUR: There's an Italian place near my apartment where I go for dinner. Or used to. One time I was there by myself and noticed a man staring at me, someone I'd never seen in my life. Coming over to my table—

HARRY: You're a literary celebrity. Wonderful. Famous for destroying my friend Jerzy.

ARTHUR: Oh...

HARRY: Basking in a glow of reflected light... What John Wilkes Booth was after. Any idea what your article has done to him?

ARTHUR: Booth?

HARRY: I'd like to throw that wine in your ratty little face.

(ARTHUR *quickly moves his wine glass away from* HARRY.)

HARRY: I'm not usually confrontational. I'm sure you don't give a shit, but I felt obliged to stroll over and let you know how thoroughly you missed the boat. As if what's "true" has any bearing. You wouldn't know a beautiful piece of writing if it beat you about the head and neck. But you're smart enough to know you've been cheated, right? You don't get it, the rest of us do. And you sense you're missing something important. Guess what, sweetheart? You are.

(ARTHUR, *out:*)

ARTHUR: He left, that's when I realized I should have told him… I'd reread *Vantage Point* maybe a week earlier. Funny timing, point is—it's a beautiful book. Inspired. *Inspiring.* But I always said it was. Always. I mean, I've gone on record— *(Beat)* Anyway, there's a French place nearby. I go there, instead.

(*A phone rings—*)

Eighteen

(GEORGIA *pulls blinds open in* JERZY's *living room. Light streams in.*)

(JERZY *enters.*)

GEORGIA: Realtor called, he's leaving keys under a fern in the back. I haven't been to the Hamptons since I was twelve. And I've never been to Gibson beach, it's supposed to be gorgeous. He said the place is ours til the 25th.

JERZY: I'm not going for three weeks.

GEORGIA: Actually you are. I'll go home and pack, you lay out clothes, books, typewriter ribbons. Please don't make me do it for you.

JERZY: Typewriter ribbons.

GEORGIA: There's a room he calls the "Captain's Office", which I assume has a view of the ocean. Or maybe it just has a maritime theme, mounted fish, one of those boats in a bottle. We'll get up early, have coffee. And you can work. Put some ideas down. I'll type if you'd rather dictate—

JERZY: *(Abruptly)* STOP!

(GEORGIA turns, but JERZY won't look at her. She goes to him.)

JERZY: *(Softly)* Sorry.

GEORGIA: No, you're right. I'm being pushy.

(Now JERZY turns.)

JERZY: You're smiling?

GEORGIA: 'Cause you're letting me in. Last night…

JERZY: You like that. Seeing me weep.

GEORGIA: I don't enjoy seeing you distressed…but you're letting yourself be vulnerable, that's a good thing. An amazing thing. I get to see past that air-tight suit of armor you wear. That's all. That's all I want. To see you.

JERZY: Peel me like an onion.

GEORGIA: 'Cause that's the end of the world, right? There's no judgment. And this is the best time to write, when you're feeling exposed. The best way to *connect…* with me, people you trust. Nothing to hide now. Can you feel that?

(Doorbell. GEORGIA hesitates, then answers it: BRETT gives her a big smile.)

BRETT: Hey! *(Then)* Wait, who are you?

GEORGIA: I'm—

BRETT: *(Spots JERZY)* Jerzy! What, is your phone unplugged? I've been calling all day.

JERZY: Brett. Didn't expect—

BRETT: Thought I'd stop in. Say hello.

JERZY: Have a seat...

BRETT: Don't think I can sit still. *(Sniffs)* Too much coffee. *(To* GEORGIA*)* Hi.

GEORGIA: Hi...

BRETT: *(To* JERZY*)* So how's things?

JERZY: Well...

BRETT: Heard you were pitching a new book.

JERZY: Mm.

BRETT: That's great.

JERZY: No one wanted it.

GEORGIA: That's not exactly—

JERZY: The big houses passed.

BRETT: Huh. A writer with your track record, you'd think...

JERZY: You would. You would think.

BRETT: What else?

GEORGIA: We're heading to the beach tomorrow.

BRETT: Sounds pleasant... What about that business with the Guild?

*(*GEORGIA *stares at* BRETT*.)*

BRETT: They decide one way or another?

JERZY: I've been ordered to give Duffy editorial credit for *Vantage Point.* His name goes on the cover with mine. And he gets a small percentage.

GEORGIA: Jerzy has the right to appeal—

JERZY: But I won't.

BRETT: Amazing. That they would do that to you. One moment you're on a pedestal, next—

GEORGIA: We're aware of the irony of the situation. Mister…?

BRETT: Sorry, I'm Brett.

GEORGIA: Georgia.

BRETT: I probably seem insensitive bringing this up. All the depressing effects of the *Voice* article.

GEORGIA: Please, can we not—

BRETT: But there's another side to this.

JERZY: What's that?

BRETT: You'd know if you'd plug in your phone. Speak to Harry recently?

JERZY: He's why it's unplugged.

(BRETT *produces a script and tosses it on the table.*)

BRETT: New deal, same people. They want to make a film.

(GEORGIA *looks at* JERZY.)

GEORGIA: *(Finally)* Wonderful…

BRETT: I think so.

JERZY: What happened to the old deal?

BRETT: *Vantage Point* is over.

JERZY: What are we talking about?

BRETT: You. We're talking about you. Your life, the whole freakish package right up to the present.

(GEORGIA *turns to* JERZY, *kisses him.*)

GEORGIA: I'll see you tomorrow, okay?

JERZY: You're going home?

GEORGIA: We'll be together all week. I'll get my bag... *(She goes into the bedroom.)*

BRETT: Please say you're interested.

JERZY: What's wrong with my book?

BRETT: A Boy Survives the War is, it's okay. But this thing with the *Voice* gives you an arc. The tragic story of a literary...I don't mean you're tragic.

JERZY: It does sound—

BRETT: They're playing with the ending. Rags to... *spiritual* riches, a revelation... You'll look like Mozart when they're done, now *he* had a fall from grace.

JERZY: Won't I look pathetic?

BRETT: You think that's what they want? A pathetic movie? It's about conflict. It can still be upbeat.

JERZY: *(Considers)* Tragic isn't bad.

BRETT: No, it's mysterious, it's...noble.

(A pause)

JERZY: I *like* tragic.

BRETT: *(Laughs)* So hell with upbeat. You go down in flames.

(Light on GEORGIA*)*

GEORGIA: It was in the paper, that the cleaning woman had found him dead in the bathtub. He'd taken a bottle of sleeping pills with a fifth of vodka and as he was dozing off, he'd wrapped a plastic bag around his head. The paper said it's what the Hemlock Society advises. The plastic bag is to ensure that you don't survive in a damaged state. *(She reenters with her bag—)*

JERZY: We've decided I'm a tragic figure.

GEORGIA: That's nice.

JERZY: You agree?

GEORGIA: No, but it's a movie. I'm sure they'll do
whatever is—

JERZY: This way I'm not hiding. You won't have to
apologize for me.

GEORGIA: What?

JERZY: This way I'm not empty. What did Arthur say?
My writing is...illusory. Layers of bright wrapping
with nothing inside.

BRETT: What a prick.

JERZY: But there *is* something inside. There is...

GEORGIA: We already know that. Something very
beautiful. *(Kisses him)* Get some sleep.

(GEORGIA starts to leave, but JERZY stops her.)

JERZY: I love you.

*(JERZY touches GEORGIA lightly on the face [as we've seen
with Kasia]).*

GEORGIA: *(Embarrassed)* I love you too...

BRETT: Nice to meet you.

(JERZY watches GEORGIA exit.)

BRETT: Take a look. *(Tosses the script over)* I'm not
supposed to admit it's been *written* until they hear
you're interested. But you are, right?

*(JERZY stares at the script. He slowly picks it up and turns a
page.)*

(Light on GEORGIA.)

GEORGIA: Since his death I'm more careful. Talking
to people. I met a woman who after ten seconds of
conversation started sharing personal stories about
herself. As a way of being friendly, I think. Only it felt
obscene.

BRETT: Opening shot. You're in front of a war memorial.

JERZY: Which one?

BRETT: The one in, I don't know. Washington. You're having a private moment, when suddenly you're cornered by a group of reporters. You try to shake them.

JERZY: I say something?

BRETT: *(Reads)* "I'm not *that* Jerzy. You're looking for a different Jerzy."

JERZY: That's the line?

(GEORGIA continues:)

GEORGIA: I never talk to anyone now. Really talk. But I'm sure I will, at some point.

JERZY: "You're looking for a different Jerzy."

BRETT: That's good...

JERZY: "I'm not that Jerzy. You're looking for a different Jerzy." *(Then)* Better?

(Lights fade leaving only JERZY, the script in his lap.)

END OF PLAY

TRANSLATION FROM POLISH

(page 11)

JERZY: *Nikt sie nie martwi co ty pamietasz.*

No one cares what you remember.

(page 12)

JERZY: *Toe sa moi przyjaciele! Rozumiesz? Nikt sie nie martwi co ty pamietasz, toe sa moi przyjaciele!*

These are my friends! Understand? No one cares what you remember, these are my friend!

(page 31)

MRS GRUSZKA: *Powiedz. Powiedz mu o Lesnewskim—*

Tell him. You tell him about Lesnewski—

MRS GRUSZKA: *Morderca.*

Murderer.

RYSIEK: *Chcialbym rozmawiac z nim osobiscie.*

I'll talk to him alone.

RYSIEK: *Hoch, hoch…*

Come, come…

(page 52)
JERZY'S FATHER: *Dlaczego nie zapytal?*
Why didn't he ask?

JERZY: *Bo wroci.*
He'll be back.

JERZY'S FATHER: *Posadz go tutaj, ja mu powiem. Ty nie jestes z nami.*
Sit him down, I will tell him. You were not with us.

(page 53)
JERZY'S FATHER: *Kiedy wroci, posadz go tu tai, ja mu powiem—*
When he comes back, sit him down here, I will tell him—

JERZY: *Prosze.*
Please.

(page 58)
RYSIEK: *Kiedy wujek byl zastrzelony czy jego ojciec byl w Dabrowie?*
When Uncle was shot, was his father in Krasnystaw?

MRS GRUSZKA: *Nie.*
No.

MRS GRUSZKA: *Ja powinnam wydac go Szwaba.*
I should have given them to the Nazis.

www.ingramcontent.com/pod-product-compliance
Lightning Source LLC
Chambersburg PA
CBHW052215090426

42741CB00010B/2555